VOLUME 15

I Know My Savior Lives

TINY
TALKS

VOLUME 15

I Know My Savior Lives

TINY TALKS

Heidi Doxey

Illustrated by Corey Egbert

CFI

An Imprint of Cedar Fort, Inc.

Springville, Utah

ISBN: 978-1-4621-1511-2

Published by CFI, an imprint of Cedar Fort, Inc.
2373 W. 700 S., Springville, Utah, 84663
www.cedarfort.com

Library of Congress Control Number: 2014951413

Front cover design by Corey Egbert
Back cover design by Shawnda T. Craig
Cover design © 2014 Lyle Mortimer
Edited and typeset by Kevin Haws

Printed in the United States of America

10 9 8 7 6 5 4 3 2 1

For Tyler, my first and favorite nephew.

Contents

Introduction

This year in Primary, we will learn about a really special person: our Savior, Jesus Christ. Jesus is our older brother, our Redeemer, and our perfect example. As we learn more about Him, we will discover how much He loves each of us and how important it is to follow His plan. He wants us to choose the right so we can return to live with Him and Heavenly Father forever. He knows we will make mistakes, but He wants us to repent and always try our best. I am excited to spend this year learning more about Jesus.

This book is a great resource when you need to write a talk for Primary—especially at the last minute—but it can also be used in family home evening lessons, sharing time, your Primary class, or for individual study. Discussing the principles and eternal truths in this book will strengthen your testimony of the Savior.

Each talk includes five different elements: a story, a scripture, a visual aid, a list of suggested illustrations, and a thought question.

STORY

Heavenly Father has given us many examples in the scriptures and in our own lives that testify of Christ's divine role. We can practice applying these examples in our own lives. This is a necessary skill for salvation, one children can learn early. The stories in this book come from the scriptures and from real life. As you read them, encourage your children to think of other stories from the scriptures that incorporate the topics in the lesson. Nephi told us that we need to "liken all scriptures unto us," and that this will benefit us and help us to learn from them (1 Nephi 19:23). Likewise, when your children give talks, always encourage them to make the talks personal by sharing how the principles they are speaking about apply to them. Encourage them to bear a simple testimony at the end of their talks.

VISUAL AID

In addition to a story, each talk includes a reference to a visual aid from the *Gospel Art Book* (GAB). This resource is available online and can be an excellent help. If you wish to purchase your own copy of the *Gospel Art Book*, it is available through Church Distribution Services. Another option is to have your children illustrate their talks.

LIST OF ILLUSTRATIONS

With each of the talks, you will find a list of suggested illustrations that complement the story. This is especially useful for children who are too young to read the talk themselves. By having your children color their own pictures of the things discussed in the talk, you will help them remember the concepts they learned as you also encourage them to share their talents. Some of these illustrations are repeated in other talks, so you may want to keep your pictures handy to use again later. This way your family can build personal art kits to use in family home evening and other settings. This will be a treasured resource and will bring back many great memories in years to come.

As a family night variation, before the lesson begins, you could have your children take turns drawing the illustrations while everyone guesses what the picture is. Once all the pictures have been drawn, have the children guess the topic of the lesson by looking at the pictures they've drawn.

THOUGHT QUESTION

Finally, each talk includes a thought question. These questions are specifically geared toward older children and teenagers, though—with perhaps a little parental prompting—they can be appropriate for young children as well. These questions will help you include your whole family in discussions and talk preparation. They can help you all to delve a little deeper into the doctrine behind each story. As you discuss these topics, make sure your children have a chance to express their thoughts. You may be surprised by how much they have already learned about the gospel and how much they can contribute.

SONG IDEAS

Another resource is the list of song ideas at the end of this book. These songs are from the *Children's Songbook*. For each tiny talk, you will find at least one song that corresponds to the themes and ideas presented that week.

For young children especially, music can be a wonderful way to reinforce and expand on key doctrinal concepts. Learning these songs when they are young will give your children a solid foundation to rely on in later years. Even if your own musical abilities are limited, you will find joy in singing with your children and in sharing with them the precious gospel truths contained in the lyrics. You can find audio and lyrics for most of these songs online at lds.org/music.

I hope you will enjoy this book and find many uses for it throughout the year. I am so grateful to all the Church leaders, family members, and friends who have taught and encouraged me. And I'm especially grateful to my Savior for His loving sacrifice that allows me to continue to learn, grow, and improve each day. I know that He lives.

I BELIEVE IN *My* HEAVENLY FATHER *and* JESUS CHRIST

"We believe in God, the Eternal Father, and in His Son, Jesus Christ, and in the Holy Ghost."—Articles of Faith 1:1

1. GOD IS MY HEAVENLY FATHER

SCRIPTURE

Take now thy son, thine only son Isaac, whom thou lovest, and get thee into the land of Moriah; and offer him there for a burnt offering.
—Genesis 22:2

VISUAL AID

GAB 9
"Abraham Taking Isaac to Be Sacrificed"

ILLUSTRATION IDEAS

Abraham, Isaac, an altar, Heavenly Father

Abraham waited a long time to have a son. He was so excited when Isaac was finally born. Then one day God told Abraham to sacrifice Isaac on an altar. Abraham didn't want to kill Isaac. He loved him so much. But Abraham knew he needed to be obedient.

Abraham prepared everything for the sacrifice. Then at the last second, an angel appeared and told Abraham that he didn't need to sacrifice Isaac after all. Both Abraham and Isaac were glad. They knew they had been blessed for being obedient. They loved each other and they knew that Heavenly Father loved them too.

Our Heavenly Father loves us even more than Abraham loved Isaac. He never wants anything bad to happen to us.

Heavenly Father is the father of your spirit. He knows who you are and how to help you. All you have to do is pray and ask for His help.

Thought Question: How does knowing that you are a child of God change your thoughts and actions?

2

2. JESUS IS GOD'S BELOVED SON

Before Jesus was born, an angel named Gabriel appeared to His mother, Mary. Gabriel said Mary would have a son and that she would name Him Jesus. Gabriel also told Mary that Jesus would be special. Mary would be His mother, but God would be His father.

Jesus is the only person to ever be born on the earth in this way. Because He is the Son of God, He was able to do many things while He was on earth that other people couldn't do. He had the power to perform miracles. He also had power over death. No one could harm Him. But He willingly died for us so He could save us from our sins.

Whenever Jesus and Heavenly Father have appeared to prophets, Heavenly Father has called Jesus His beloved Son. This means that Heavenly Father loves Jesus and He knows how good Jesus is. He wants us to follow Jesus's example so we can become like Him.

Thought Question: What other things can Jesus do because He is the Son of God?

SCRIPTURE

And the angel said unto her, Fear not, Mary: for thou hast found favour with God. And, behold, thou shalt conceive in thy womb, and bring forth a son, and shalt call his name Jesus. —Luke 1:30–31

VISUAL AID

GAB 28
"The Annunciation: The Angel Gabriel Appears to Mary"

ILLUSTRATION IDEAS

Gabriel, Mary, Jesus, Heavenly Father

3. MY HEAVENLY FATHER LOVES ME

SCRIPTURE

And I, God, saw everything that I had made, and, behold, all things which I had made were very good.
—Moses 2:31

VISUAL AID

GAB 3
"The Earth"

ILLUSTRATION IDEAS

A bird, a nest, a frog, a dinosaur, the earth, Heavenly Father

Most birds build nests before they lay their eggs. But did you know many other animals build nests too? Insects and alligators build nests. So do gorillas and certain kinds of frogs. Even dinosaurs built nests.

A nest is a safe place for a baby animal to be born in and grow up. Heavenly Father created a nest for us too. It is this earth. Heavenly Father and Jesus knew that we needed a safe place to learn how to become like Them. They designed this beautiful world for us with wonderful things to see and smell and hear.

We can remember how much Heavenly Father loves us when we see the beautiful world we live in. We can see His love when we remember that He sent us to live with people who love us.

Even though Heavenly Father lives far away, He still loves us and wants to bless us every day.

Thought Question: What specific things testify of God's love to you?

4. JESUS IS MY LOVING BROTHER

Charlotte's brother, James, is autistic. Sometimes it's hard for James to understand other people. But even when he gets frustrated, Charlotte knows James still loves her. Just because he can't show it doesn't mean the love isn't there.

Charlotte has another brother. His name is Jesus Christ, and He is your brother too. Even though Jesus doesn't live in your house, He is your older brother and He loves you.

We know Jesus loves us because He made this world for us. He showed us how to choose the right. He even died for us. And because He died and was resurrected, He knows exactly how to help us return to Heavenly Father.

Sometimes it can be hard to see how much Jesus loves us because He isn't here with us. But even though He's not here, His love is still all around us.

Thought Question: How can you recognize the Savior's loving presence in your life?

SCRIPTURE

I am the first and the last; I am he who liveth, I am he who was slain; I am your advocate with the Father.
—D&C 110:4

VISUAL AID

GAB 116
"Christ and Children from around the World"

ILLUSTRATION IDEAS

A girl, a boy, a heart, Jesus, the earth, Heavenly Father

CHAPTER 2

JESUS PERFORMED *the* ATONEMENT *for* ME

"For God so loved the world, that he gave his only begotten Son, that whosoever believeth in him should not perish, but have everlasting life."—John 3:16

1. JESUS SAVED AND REDEEMED ME

SCRIPTURE

For behold, I, God, have suffered these things for all, that they might not suffer if they would repent.
—D&C 19:16

VISUAL AID

GAB 56
"Jesus Praying in Gethsemane"

ILLUSTRATION IDEAS

A girl, a mom, a grocery store, coupons, Jesus

Carolyn likes to go grocery shopping with her mom. When they get to the checkout counter, Carolyn helps by giving the cashier all their coupons. When we use a coupon, we sometimes say we're redeeming that coupon, meaning we get something for free or for less money because someone else already paid for it.

So what does it mean when we say Jesus redeemed us? It means we don't have to pay the price for our sins because He already paid for them. Any time we make a mistake, we can repent and Jesus will pay the price.

This doesn't that mean we should make mistakes on purpose just because we can repent. But it does mean that there is almost nothing we can do that He can't fix. Jesus knows we will make mistakes, but He never wants us to feel discouraged. He paid for our sins so that we could always have a way to return to Him and be happy.

Thought Question: What are some things you need to do in order to repent?

2. JESUS ATONED FOR MY SINS

One time, some people brought a man to Jesus. They wanted Jesus to heal the man because he had a sickness called palsy. The man couldn't walk, so his friends had carried him to see Jesus. Both the man and his friends had faith. They knew Jesus could heal him.

Jesus saw their faith. He wanted to help the man. He told the man to be happy and that the man's sins were forgiven. Some other people who were there got angry. They didn't think Jesus could forgive sins. They thought that was something only God could do.

Jesus does have the power to forgive sins. When He died, He suffered for all the sins and bad feelings we've ever had or will have. The people watching didn't understand this. So Jesus showed them His power. He told the sick man to stand up and walk. And the man did. Jesus healed his body and his spirit at the same time.

Thought Question: The Atonement covers more than just our sins. What else does it help us with?

SCRIPTURE

And Jesus seeing their faith said unto the sick of the palsy; Son, be of good cheer; thy sins be forgiven thee. —Matthew 9:2

VISUAL AID

GAB 54
"The Last Supper"

ILLUSTRATION IDEAS

Jesus, a sick man, some angry people

3. THE ATONEMENT IS FOR EVERYONE

SCRIPTURE

We believe that through the Atonement of Christ, all mankind may be saved, by obedience to the laws and ordinances of the Gospel.
—Articles of Faith 1:3

VISUAL AID

GAB 57
"The Crucifixion"

ILLUSTRATION IDEAS

Some different church buildings, Jesus, lots of people, heaven

Every church is different. Some churches believe that after we die we're gone forever. Other churches believe we are born again as a new person on the earth. And some churches believe in Jesus, but they think only a few special people will get to live in heaven after they die.

In our Church, we know that when Jesus died, He did it for everyone. All of the people who have ever lived on earth have had bodies. And all of them will have perfect resurrected bodies again someday. That's because the Atonement works for good and bad people.

Then, after we are resurrected, almost everyone will be able to live in a heavenly place that is better than anything we can imagine. The best people will live with Heavenly Father and Jesus, but everyone will be in a place where they can be happy. That's because Jesus loves everyone and He died to save all of us.

Thought Question: What are the differences between the three kingdoms of glory?

4. HE LIVES AND SO WILL I

After Jesus died, He appeared to the Apostles. But one of them—Thomas—wasn't there. The other Apostles told Thomas what had happened, but he didn't believe them. He hoped Jesus was alive again, but he needed to see for himself.

It can be hard to believe in things you can't see. Most of us will never see Jesus while we are alive. But we can know He lives and He loves us. The Holy Ghost can tell our spirits things our minds can't understand yet.

Later, Jesus appeared to Thomas and he became a witness of Jesus. We have many witnesses that Jesus was resurrected. The scriptures are one witness. So are our latter-day prophets. But the most important witness is the one your spirit receives when you pray with faith. Knowing Jesus lives is so important because His Resurrection made it so we can live again too.

Thought Question: How do you learn things with your mind and how do you learn things with your spirit?

SCRIPTURE

Jesus saith unto him, Thomas, because thou hast seen me, thou hast believed: blessed are they that have not seen, and yet have believed. —John 20:29

VISUAL AID

GAB 60 "Jesus Shows His Wounds"

ILLUSTRATION IDEAS

Jesus, the Apostles, Thomas, the scriptures, a prophet, the Holy Ghost

CHAPTER 3

HEAVENLY FATHER *Calls* PROPHETS *to* HELP HIM

"He spake by the mouth of his holy prophets, which have been since the world began."—Luke 1:70

1. HEAVENLY FATHER CALLS PROPHETS

SCRIPTURE

And when the sons of the prophets . . . saw him, they said, The spirit of Elijah doth rest on Elisha.
—2 Kings 2:13

VISUAL AID

GAB 20
"Elijah Contends against the Priests of Baal"

ILLUSTRATION IDEAS

Elisha, Elijah, a river, Elijah's coat, Heavenly Father

Elisha was friends with the prophet Elijah. One day, the Lord told them to go to Jordan. To get there, they had to cross a river. Elijah performed a miracle. He hit the water with his coat, and the river parted so they could walk across. Many people watched Elijah do this.

When they got to Jordan, Elijah was translated. This means he went to live with Heavenly Father. The Lord said Elisha would be the new prophet. Elisha obeyed the Lord. He took Elijah's coat back to the river and used it to part the river, just as Elijah had done. All the people who saw this knew Elisha was the new prophet. It wasn't up to the people to decide. The Lord had already chosen Elisha.

This is the same way Heavenly Father calls prophets today. It's not up to other people to decide. Heavenly Father already knows who the prophet should be and He chooses the right person.

Thought Question: Why is it important to let Heavenly Father choose who the prophet should be?

2. A PROPHET TEACHES ABOUT JESUS

Samuel was a Lamanite prophet who had learned a lot about Jesus. He lived in a time when many people were wicked. But Samuel knew what was right. He tried to teach the people around him. One time, he climbed on top of a wall so more people could hear him. Samuel said that Jesus would soon be born far away.

Righteous people like Samuel had waited a long time for Jesus to be born. They were really excited. But the wicked people didn't believe in Jesus. They wanted to hurt Samuel.

The wicked people shot arrows at Samuel and threw stones at him. But Jesus protected Samuel. None of the arrows or stones hit him.

Every prophet teaches about Jesus, just like Samuel did. Sometimes it's not easy to teach wicked people, but Jesus protects His prophets and followers.

Thought Question: What are some specific things that Samuel prophesied about Jesus?

SCRIPTURE

There were many who heard the words of Samuel, the Lamanite, which he spake upon the walls of the city. And as many as believed on his word went forth . . . that they might be baptized.
—Helaman 16:1

VISUAL AID

GAB 81
"Samuel the Lamanite on the Wall"

ILLUSTRATION IDEAS

Samuel, a wall, some angry people, arrows, stones, Jesus

3. I CAN BE SAFE WHEN I FOLLOW THE PROPHET

SCRIPTURE

Give heed unto all his words and commandments which he shall give unto you as he receiveth them, walking in all holiness before me; for his word ye shall receive, as if from mine own mouth.
—D&C 21:4–5

VISUAL AID

GAB 67
"Lehi Prophesying to the People of Jerusalem"

ILLUSTRATION IDEAS

A boy, a boat, water, a life jacket, a flag, a prophet

Jaxon's family likes to go boating together. When they are out on the water, Jaxon knows he needs to follow the rules so he can be safe. Everyone on the boat wears a life jacket. And Jaxon helps by holding up a flag to send messages to other boats nearby.

Prophets teach us the rules that keep us safe in life. They show us how to stay close to the Spirit. The Spirit is like a life jacket. It can keep us safe from bad thoughts or bad habits. A prophet will never tell us to do something bad or wrong. When we follow the prophet and stay close to the Spirit, we can be happy and feel peace.

Jaxon loves to go boating with his family. And he loves to follow the prophet. He knows that when he obeys the rules and keeps the commandments, he can have fun without worrying. When Jaxon is obedient, he can always have the Spirit with him and be safe.

Thought Question: How many prophets can you name from the scriptures and the latter days?

4. WHEN I LISTEN TO THE PROPHETS, I AM LISTENING TO GOD

There are many different kinds of musical instruments. Can you think of some? There are pianos, drums, and guitars. And there are instruments you play by blowing into them, like trumpets and flutes. Most instruments you blow into have a certain part on them that's called a mouthpiece. It's the part of the instrument that goes in the player's mouth. The mouthpiece helps to turn the player's breath into music for people to enjoy.

Sometimes we call a prophet the mouthpiece of the Lord. This is because prophets help turn revelation from the Lord into rules and commandments that will allow us to be happy if we follow them.

When you listen to a prophet, it's like you are listening to Heavenly Father Himself. The things our prophet tells us to do can help us enjoy our lives here and return to live with Heavenly Father someday.

Thought Question: What are some things the prophet has told us to do recently?

SCRIPTURE

What I the Lord have spoken, I have spoken, and I excuse not myself . . . my word shall not pass away, but shall all be fulfilled, whether by mine own voice or by the voice of my servants, it is the same. —D&C 1:38

VISUAL AID

GAB 137
"Thomas S. Monson"

ILLUSTRATION IDEAS

A trumpet or flute, a prophet, the conference center

CHAPTER 4

JOSEPH SMITH RESTORED *the* GOSPEL

"We believe in the same organization that existed in the Primitive Church."—Articles of Faith 1:6

1. JOSEPH SMITH SAW GOD AND JESUS

SCRIPTURE

If any of you lack wisdom, let him ask of God, that giveth to all men liberally, and upbraideth not; and it shall be given him.
—James 1:5

VISUAL AID

GAB 89
"Joseph Smith Seeks Wisdom in the Bible"

ILLUSTRATION IDEAS

Joseph Smith, the scriptures, Heavenly Father, Jesus

When Joseph Smith was young, he was curious. He wanted to know which church was right. He spent many years going to different churches to try them out. He also read the scriptures and learned all he could on his own.

One day, as he was reading, he found a verse in the book of James that told him what to do. It said that if you want to know the truth about something, you should ask God. Joseph knew that God was the only one who could answer his questions about which church was right.

So Joseph prayed. To his surprise, both God and Jesus appeared to him. They told him that none of the churches were completely right and that Joseph would be the one to bring the right church back to the earth.

We are blessed to have prophets who can speak with God and tell us what we need to know today. And it all started with Joseph Smith and his one simple prayer.

Thought Question: What specific things did Joseph Smith learn from the First Vision?

2. JOSEPH SMITH USED GOD'S POWER TO TRANSLATE THE BOOK OF MORMON

One day, the power went out at Carter and Savannah's house. They had to turn on flashlights and light candles to see when it got dark out. And they couldn't use their microwave or TV or computer. It was strange.

Electricity helps us to do lots of important things. But God has another kind of power He uses. It is called the priesthood. The priesthood aids us in many ways. When we are sick or sad, the priesthood can help us feel better.

Joseph Smith used priesthood power to translate the Book of Mormon. With God's help, he could read the record out loud so another person could write the words down. Joseph could not do this alone. He needed to use the priesthood.

We are blessed to have the Book of Mormon and to have God's priesthood power on the earth for us to use righteously.

Thought Question: Who was a scribe for Joseph Smith when he translated the Book of Mormon?

SCRIPTURE

And gave him power from on high, by the means which were before prepared, to translate the Book of Mormon.
—D&C 20:8

VISUAL AID

GAB 92
"Joseph Smith Translating the Book of Mormon"

ILLUSTRATION IDEAS

A flashlight, a candle, a TV, Joseph Smith, the Book of Mormon

3. JESUS WANTS EVERYONE TO KNOW THE TRUTH

SCRIPTURE

And as I partook of the fruit thereof it filled my soul with exceedingly great joy; wherefore, I began to be desirous that my family should partake of it also.
—1 Nephi 8:12

VISUAL AID

GAB 69
"Lehi's Dream"

ILLUSTRATION IDEAS

Lehi, a tree, fruit, Jesus, Joseph Smith, a missionary

Lehi had an important dream. He dreamed about a tree with yummy fruit on it that made him happy. After Lehi ate some of the fruit on the tree, the first thing he wanted to do was share the fruit with his family. He wanted them to be as happy as he was. Some of Lehi's family came and ate the fruit with him. But others did not.

In Lehi's dream, the fruit was a symbol for the Savior's love and the truth of the gospel. The Savior wants everyone to have a chance to know His truth. That is why He helped Joseph Smith restore the true gospel in our day. When we learn about the Savior's love and the gospel, we get to share what we know with those around us.

Some people will be happy to hear the truth. Others might not understand how important it is. That's okay. Our job is to keep sharing the gospel with everyone so they have the chance to be as happy as we are.

Thought Question: Who were some of the first missionaries to share the restored gospel in our day?

4. JOSEPH SMITH HELPED RESTORE THE GOSPEL IN OUR DAY

Weston's family is working on a big project, and it's taking a long time. They're restoring an old house so they can live there. Sometimes it's hard to imagine what it will look like when it's done. But each time they work on the house, whether they're painting or taking out rotten wood, Weston knows they're getting closer to finishing.

When Joseph Smith restored the gospel, it took him a long time too. Sometimes he had to make big changes and take out old teachings that had become rotten or warped—like the wood in Weston's house.

It was hard for Joseph's friends to understand why things needed to change. They couldn't imagine what the gospel would be like when it was fully restored. But Joseph knew Heavenly Father had a plan. Now that the gospel has been fully restored, we know exactly how to return to live with our Heavenly Father.

Thought Question: Why did the gospel need to be restored in our day?

SCRIPTURE

So it was with me. I had actually seen a light, and in the midst of that light I saw two Personages . . . and though I was hated and persecuted for saying that I had seen a vision, yet it was true.
—Joseph Smith—History 1:25

VISUAL AID

GAB 87
"Brother Joseph"

ILLUSTRATION IDEAS

A boy, a house, some old wood, Joseph Smith, Heavenly Father

CHAPTER 5

PRINCIPLES *and* ORDINANCES HELP ME BECOME *like* JESUS

"We believe that the first principles and ordinances of the Gospel are: first, Faith in the Lord Jesus Christ; second, Repentance; third, Baptism by immersion for the remission of sins; fourth, Laying on of hands for the gift of the Holy Ghost."—Articles of Faith 1:4

1. WHEN I AM OBEDIENT, I LEARN MORE ABOUT JESUS

SCRIPTURE

Suffer the little children to come unto me, and forbid them not: for of such is the kingdom of God.
—Mark 10:14

Madalyn is learning to read. She just started reading chapter books all by herself! Madalyn loves to learn new things every time she reads a new book.

But Madalyn knows that there are other ways to learn too. We can learn by watching other people do things and then trying to copy them. And we can also learn by teaching someone else how to do something.

We don't need to know how to read in order to learn about Jesus. All we need to do is copy His example by doing the things He would do if He were here. Jesus loved everyone, so we should love others and be kind. Jesus forgave, so we should forgive other people and ourselves. Jesus helped His family, so we should help our families. Every time we do something Jesus would do, we learn a little bit more about Him. Then we can teach others how to become like Him too.

Thought Question: How can you teach others to be more like Jesus?

VISUAL AID

GAB 36
"Jesus and the Samaritan Woman"

ILLUSTRATION IDEAS

A girl, a book, Jesus, a heart, a family

2. MY SPIRIT GROWS WHEN I REPENT

On the wall in Quinton's room is a chart that shows how tall he is. The chart is marked with dates. As Quinton has grown up, he has gotten taller and taller. You can tell by the marks on his chart.

Quinton's spirit is growing too. We can't see our spirits growing the same way we can see our bodies grow. But each time we choose the right, our spirits grow a little more. When we make mistakes, our spirits can't grow until we repent.

We repent by admitting that we did something wrong and then trying to make it right. We also need to ask Heavenly Father to forgive us.

Because Heavenly Father loves us, He made it so that we can repent. He wants our spirits to keep growing, and He knows that learning how to repent is the best way for us to keep our spirits healthy and strong.

Thought Question: What are some things you might want to repent of so your spirit can keep growing?

SCRIPTURE

For behold, this life is the time for men to prepare to meet God; yea, behold the day of this life is the day for men to perform their labors.
—Alma 34:32

VISUAL AID

GAB 56
"Jesus Praying in Gethsemane"

ILLUSTRATION IDEAS

A boy, a growth chart, a spirit, Heavenly Father

27

3. BAPTISM IS A COVENANT WITH GOD

SCRIPTURE

And I will remember my covenant, which is between me and you.
—Genesis 9:15

VISUAL AID

GAB 8
"Noah and the Ark with Animals"

ILLUSTRATION IDEAS

Noah, the ark, animals, Heavenly Father, a baptismal font

God gave Noah an important job. He told Noah to build a huge boat called an ark because soon there would be a flood. God wanted Noah to save all the animals and righteous people. Noah worked hard on the ark. Then he gathered all the animals and put them inside. When the flood came, Noah and the animals and those that were righteous were safe in the ark.

It rained for a long time. The flood covered the whole earth. After it ended, God made a promise with Noah that He would never have a flood like that again.

God still makes promises today. They are called covenants and they work in two ways: God promises to do things for us and we promise to do things for Him.

Baptism is one of the covenants we make with God. When we are baptized, we promise to help others and keep the commandments. In return, God promises to bless us and give us the Holy Ghost.

Thought Question: Do you know any other covenants?

4. I RECEIVE THE HOLY GHOST WHEN I AM CONFIRMED

When Jesus lived on the earth, He called the Apostles to help Him with His work. The Apostles spent a lot of time with Jesus. They loved to be around Him because He was so loving and wise. He taught them many things.

But Jesus knew He would soon have to die. He told His Apostles that His work was almost done and that He would be going back to live with Heavenly Father.

The Apostles were sad. They loved Jesus. They didn't want Him to leave them alone. But Jesus said they wouldn't be alone. He said He would give them the Holy Ghost.

The Holy Ghost is a member of the godhead, like Jesus. But the Holy Ghost doesn't have a body. That meant the Holy Ghost could stay with the Apostles all the time. And it means He can still stay with us today. Each of us receives the gift of the Holy Ghost when we are confirmed. The Holy Ghost can comfort us and teach us many things, just like Jesus would do if He were here.

Thought Question: What is the difference between the Holy Ghost and a conscience?

SCRIPTURE

And I will pray the Father, and he shall give you another Comforter, that he may abide with you for ever; even the Spirit of truth.
—John 14:16–17

VISUAL AID

GAB 61
"Go Ye Therefore"

ILLUSTRATION IDEAS

Jesus, the apostles, Heavenly Father, the Holy Ghost

CHAPTER 6

The HOLY GHOST REVEALS TRUTH

"By the power of the Holy Ghost ye may know the truth of all things."—Moroni 10:5

1. GOD, JESUS, AND THE HOLY GHOST MAKE UP THE GODHEAD

SCRIPTURE

The Father has a body of flesh and bones as tangible as man's; the Son also; but the Holy Ghost has not a body of flesh and bones, but is a personage of Spirit.
—D&C 130:22

VISUAL AID

GAB 137
"Thomas S. Monson"

ILLUSTRATION IDEAS

President Monson with his counselors, Heavenly Father, Jesus, the Holy Ghost

President Monson is our prophet today. He has two counselors who help him. Do you know their names? A bishop has two counselors too. In fact, there are many groups in our Church that have three leaders who work together.

That's what the Godhead is like. Heavenly Father is in charge. He leads the way, and Jesus and the Holy Ghost are His helpers. All three of Them work together to do all the wonderful things They do for us. They worked together to create the earth and They still work together to help us all return to live with Them eternally.

We are so blessed because we can have a member of the Godhead with us all the time. When we feel the Holy Ghost, we are feeling what it's like to be with Jesus and Heavenly Father.

Thought Question: Have you ever felt the Holy Ghost? What did it feel like to you?

2. THE HOLY GHOST CAN TALK TO ME

Cecil has a great imagination. He likes to pretend that he's a firefighter or a dinosaur hunter or a pirate. Sometimes he pretends that his mom's car is a rocket ship. Cecil likes to use his imagination and play pretend games. He can't really see the things that he imagines, but to Cecil they are real.

We can't see the Holy Ghost either, but we don't have to pretend that He is there. The Holy Ghost is real. And He can talk to us just like our friends do. We just need to learn how to listen to Him. The Holy Ghost can tell us things in our minds and in our hearts. He talks to our spirits when we are quiet.

You will know the Holy Ghost is there when you feel happy about who you are and what you're choosing to do. If you really want to hear Him, the Holy Ghost will always be there.

Thought Question: Why do you think the Holy Ghost speaks in a still, small voice instead of a loud one?

SCRIPTURE

Yea, behold, I will tell you in your mind and in your heart, by the Holy Ghost, which shall come upon you and . . . dwell in your heart.
—D&C 8:2

VISUAL AID

GAB 105
"The Gift of the Holy Ghost"

ILLUSTRATION IDEAS

A boy, a firefighter, a dinosaur, a pirate, the Holy Ghost

3. I CAN FOLLOW THE SPIRIT'S VOICE

SCRIPTURE

And they heard the voice of
the Lord God
walking in the garden.
—Genesis 3:8

When Adam and Eve lived in the Garden of Eden, God visited them and talked with them. But after they ate the fruit that God had told them not to eat, Adam and Eve had to leave the garden. God couldn't visit them anymore. Instead, Adam and Eve had to learn how to hear the Spirit's voice. Then Adam and Eve taught their children how to hear it too.

It's been a long time since Adam and Eve were alive, but the Spirit still speaks to us in the same way He did to them.

The Spirit's voice is still and small. You can't hear it if you are being loud or if you're busy. You have to learn how to be still and quiet. Praying and reading the scriptures can help. When you listen, the Spirit can teach you all the things that God wants you to know.

Thought Question: How can you know if a prompting is from the Spirit or if it's just something you thought up on your own?

VISUAL AID

GAB 5
"Adam and Eve Teaching
Their Children"

ILLUSTRATION IDEAS

Adam and Eve, the garden of
Eden, God, the Holy Ghost

4. I KNOW THE TRUTH BECAUSE OF THE HOLY GHOST

Max's favorite TV show is about a detective. In every episode, the detective tries to figure out the clues of the case to learn what really happened. The detective wants to find out the truth.

Max knows how to find out what is true. He doesn't need to be a detective. He just needs the Holy Ghost.

One of the Holy Ghost's most important jobs is to testify of truth. This means that if we want to know the truth, we can pray and the Holy Ghost will help us know. That's how Joseph Smith knew the truth about which church to join. And it's how you can know the truth too.

All you have to do is think hard about something. This is called pondering. Then you need to pray and ask if it's true. If it is true, the Holy Ghost will help you feel good about that thing and you will know that it's true.

Thought Question: Can you think of any other scripture stories about people who prayed to know the truth?

SCRIPTURE

And now I do know of myself that they are true; for the Lord God hath made them manifest unto me by his Holy Spirit; and this is the spirit of revelation which is in me. —Alma 5:46

VISUAL AID

GAB 111 "Young Boy Praying"

ILLUSTRATION IDEAS

A boy, a detective, the Holy Ghost, Joseph Smith

CHAPTER 7

JESUS IS *My* PERFECT EXAMPLE

"Now when Jesus heard these things, he said . . .
come, follow me."—Luke 18:22

1. JESUS LIVED PERFECTLY

SCRIPTURE

Therefore I would that ye should be perfect even as I, or your father who is in heaven is perfect.
—3 Nephi 12:48

VISUAL AID

GAB 50
"Triumphal Entry"

ILLUSTRATION IDEAS

A girl, a mom, crayons or markers, Jesus, Heavenly Father

Chloe decided to draw a picture for her mother. She wanted it to be perfect. She chose just the right colors and took a long time trying to get it right. But no matter how much she tried, Chloe couldn't seem to get the picture she was drawing to match the perfect one she imagined.

That's how our lives are too. Most people want to be good. They imagine themselves being perfect and never making any mistakes. But no matter how hard we try to always choose the right, we all make mistakes.

Except for Jesus. He is the only one who lived a perfect life. Jesus never made any mistakes. He always did exactly what Heavenly Father wanted Him to do.

And because Jesus was perfect, we know that when we follow His example, we will be doing exactly what our Heavenly Father wants us to do. That's why it's important to learn about Jesus and try to follow Him.

Thought Question: Is it possible for anyone to become perfect without Jesus? Why or why not?

2. JESUS LOVED AND HELPED OTHERS

Jesus taught us how to love others. When He lived on the earth, there were many different groups of people who didn't like each other. Lots of people didn't like the Samaritans, but Jesus loved them anyway. Many people didn't like tax collectors, but Jesus chose a tax collector to be one of His Apostles. Jesus loved everyone, even when they were making bad choices.

One time, some people brought a woman to Jesus. The woman had been caught doing something wrong. The people wanted Jesus to get mad at her. But Jesus knew the woman already felt bad about what had happened. He told the people to leave her alone. Then he helped the woman feel better.

Jesus commanded us to love everyone, just like He did. He doesn't want us to judge people. He just wants us to help them, no matter what.

Thought Question: Have you ever judged someone and then found out you were wrong about them?

SCRIPTURE

He said unto her, Woman, where are those thine accusers? hath no man condemned thee? She said, No man, Lord. And Jesus said unto her, Neither do I condemn thee: go, and sin no more. —John 8:10–11

VISUAL AID

GAB 55
"Jesus Washing the Apostles' Feet"

ILLUSTRATION IDEAS

Jesus, a heart, a woman

3. I CAN FOLLOW CHRIST'S EXAMPLE

SCRIPTURE

For I have given you an example, that ye should do as I have done to you.
—John 13:15

VISUAL AID

GAB 64
"Jesus Carrying a Lost Lamb"

ILLUSTRATION IDEAS

Three sisters, a movie theater, a restaurant, Jesus

Sierra and Kylie have an older sister named Jessica. The three of them love to spend time together. Jessica takes them to do fun things like go to the movies or get a treat from their favorite restaurant. Jessica is a great older sister. She takes good care of Sierra and Kylie.

Both Sierra and Kylie look up to Jessica because she is their sister. They want to follow her example and be just like her someday.

Each of us has an older brother we can look up to. Jesus is our older brother. He takes good care of us because He loves us and wants us to be happy.

We should try to follow the example our older brother gave us. When we need to make a choice, we should think about what Jesus might do. Choosing the right helps us return to Jesus and Heavenly Father so we can be happy living with them forever.

Thought Question: Which of Jesus's qualities could you focus on so you can become more like Him?

4. WHEN I FOLLOW JESUS, I AM HAPPY

Holland is only three, but he is learning lots of things. He's learning how to write his name and how to color pictures with crayons. He's learning how to do puzzles and swim in the pool. And he's learning how to get dressed all by himself and make his own snacks.

And even though he's little, Holland is also learning something important. He's learning how to follow Jesus. Holland's parents know how important it is to follow Jesus's example. Following Him helps us be happy, and Holland's parents want Holland to know how to be happy.

As a family, they are reading stories about Jesus and teaching Holland who He is. That way Holland can learn to choose the things Jesus would choose. It is important to learn how to follow Jesus when you are young because then you can start making good choices early and be happy for your whole life.

Thought Question: What are some gospel habits you can start when you're young and keep your whole life?

SCRIPTURE

What manner of men ought ye to be? Verily I say unto you, even as I am.
—3 Nephi 27:27

VISUAL AID

GAB 39
"The Sermon on the Mount"

ILLUSTRATION IDEAS

A boy, crayons, clothes, a snack, Jesus

CHAPTER 8

I WANT *to* LEARN *about* JESUS

"For behold, I am God; and I am a God of miracles; . . . and I work not among the children of men save it be according to their faith."—2 Nephi 27:23

1. JESUS PERFORMS MIRACLES

SCRIPTURE

Go thou to the sea, and cast an hook, and take up the fish that first cometh up; and when thou hast opened his mouth, thou shalt find a piece of money.
—Matthew 17:27

VISUAL AID

GAB 37
"Calling of the Fishermen"

ILLUSTRATION IDEAS

Peter, some men, Jesus, a fish, a coin

One time, some men came to Peter. The men said that Jesus needed to pay them money. Peter wasn't sure what to do, so he went to talk to Jesus. Jesus told Peter how to find money for the men.

He said that Peter should go to the sea and do some fishing. Jesus said that when Peter caught his first fish, he should open the fish's mouth and there would be a coin inside. Peter did as Jesus told him. He found a coin, just like Jesus said he would. Peter gave the coin to the men.

This was a miracle. Jesus performed lots of miracles while He was on earth. Because He was God's son, Jesus could do things no one else could. He had God's power.

Miracles still happen today. That's because we have the priesthood. The priesthood is God's power. It is the same power Jesus used to perform miracles when he was alive.

Thought Question: Who do you know that holds the priesthood?

2. JESUS HEALED SICK PEOPLE

When Jesus was in Jerusalem, he walked past a place where there was a pool of water. Lots of sick people were gathered around the pool because they thought that the water could help them get better.

One of the men there had been sick almost his whole life. Jesus asked the man if the man wanted to be healed. The man said he did want to be healed, but he had no one to help him get to the water. The man couldn't get better on his own. He needed someone's help.

Jesus told the man he didn't need the water to heal him. All the man needed was to have faith. Jesus then told the man to get up and walk, and he did. Jesus had healed him.

The man was so grateful to Jesus. He told everyone how he had been healed. Many people who saw this miracle happen began to believe in Jesus's power too.

Thought Question: How does Jesus continue to heal people today through the power of the Atonement?

SCRIPTURE

Jesus saith unto him, Rise, take up thy bed, and walk. And immediately the man was made whole, and took up his bed, and walked.
—John 5:8–9

VISUAL AID

GAB 42
"Christ Healing the Sick at Bethesda"

ILLUSTRATION IDEAS

A sick man, a pool of water, Jesus

3. JESUS RAISED THE DEAD

SCRIPTURE

And he put them all out, and took her by the hand, and called, saying, Maid, arise. And her spirit came again, and she arose straightway.
—Luke 8:54–55

VISUAL AID

GAB 41
"Jesus Raising Jairus's Daughter"

ILLUSTRATION IDEAS

Jesus, Jairus, Jairus's daughter

When Jesus lived on the earth, he traveled to lots of places, performing miracles and teaching people what Heavenly Father wanted them to know. After a while, lots of people knew about Jesus. They came to Him and asked Him to work miracles for them too.

One time, a man named Jairus came to Jesus to ask for help. Jairus said his daughter was about to die. Jesus agreed to help. When they got there, Jairus's daughter had already died. Jesus told everyone not to worry.

All of the people laughed at Jesus. They said there was nothing He could do because the girl was already dead. But Jesus knew He could still help. He went into the house and commanded Jairus's daughter to get up. And she did. Jesus had the power to bring her back to life. All of the people were amazed at this miracle.

Thought Question: Why do you think it's hard for some people to believe that miracles still happen?

4. MIRACLES ONLY HAPPEN WHEN WE HAVE FAITH

Moroni knew how important it was to have faith. He liked to read the scriptures, especially the stories about righteous people and the miracles they got to see. In the Book of Mormon, Moroni tells us that miracles only happen when we have faith first.

Moroni said it was through faith that many things happened. Christ showed himself to the Nephites after He was resurrected because they had faith. Moses received the Ten Commandments because he had faith. The prison that Alma and Amulek were in fell down and they were freed because they had faith. Ammon was able to teach the Lamanites because he had faith. And the brother of Jared saw Jesus because he had faith.

Miracles still happen in our day. But before a miracle can happen, we have to have faith.

Thought Question: Have you ever witnessed a miracle in your life? What was it like?

SCRIPTURE

Yea, and even all they who wrought miracles wrought them by faith.
—Ether 12:16

VISUAL AID

GAB 86
"Moroni Hides the Plates in the Hill Cumorah"

ILLUSTRATION IDEAS

Moroni, Jesus, Moses, a prison, Ammon, the brother of Jared

CHAPTER 9

WHEN I *Am* OBEDIENT, I SHOW JESUS *That* I LOVE HIM

"If ye love me, keep my commandments."—John 14:15

1. JESUS GAVE ME COMMANDMENTS

SCRIPTURE

Ye have heard that it was said by them of old time, Thou shalt not kill. . . . But I say unto you, that whosoever is angry with his brother without a cause shall be in danger of the judgment.
—Matthew 5:21–22

VISUAL AID

GAB 14
"The Ten Commandments"

ILLUSTRATION IDEAS

A boy and girl, a bike, a road, the Ten Commandments, Jesus

Ethan and Hannah love to ride their bikes together. They know that when they're riding, it's important to follow some special rules. They need to wear helmets and stop at stop signs. They also need to stay on the sidewalk or in the bike lane. And they need to go slowly around other people so they don't hurt anyone.

The commandments are special rules too. They help us to stay safe and they keep us from getting hurt or from hurting other people. The commandments tell us what kinds of things we should or should not do. Jesus explained that we also need to be careful about the things we think about and the things we say.

Jesus gave us commandments because He loves us and wants us to be happy. He knows that when we obey the commandments, we will be blessed.

Thought Question: Can you remember all of the Ten Commandments?

2. WHEN I OBEY THE COMMANDMENTS, I'M SHOWING JESUS THAT I LOVE HIM

King Benjamin taught that Jesus gives us so many things it's impossible to ever pay him back. But King Benjamin also said that the one thing we can do for Jesus is keep the commandments.

When we are obedient and choose the right, we show Jesus that we love Him. It's nice to tell Jesus that you love Him, but it's more important to show Him that you mean it. You can show your love for Jesus by being kind to others, paying your tithing, and obeying the Word of Wisdom. You can also show your love by only watching good media and reading your scriptures and other good books.

Jesus loves us so much. He has given us so many blessings. He wants us to be happy and He knows that obeying the commandments will help us to be happier than we could ever be without them.

Thought Question: Why did King Benjamin call us "unprofitable servants" (Mosiah 2:21)?

SCRIPTURE

And behold, all that he requires of you is to keep his commandments.
—Mosiah 2:22

VISUAL AID

GAB 74
"King Benjamin Addresses His People"

ILLUSTRATION IDEAS

King Benjamin, Jesus, a tithing envelope, the scriptures

3. I LOVE JESUS MORE WHEN I PRAY

SCRIPTURE

For the space of three hours did the Lord talk with the brother of Jared, and chastened him because he remembered not to call upon the name of the Lord.
—Ether 2:14

VISUAL AID

GAB 85
"The Brother of Jared Sees the Finger of the Lord"

ILLUSTRATION IDEAS

The brother of Jared, the sea, Jesus, a heart

The brother of Jared was a good man. When the people around him started making bad choices, he led his family and friends away. Jesus told the brother of Jared to take all the good people to the promised land, so they traveled until they reached the sea.

Four years passed. The people were happy where they were, but they had not yet reached the promised land. Then one day, Jesus visited the brother of Jared. Jesus was upset because the brother of Jared had been forgetting to pray. Jesus told the brother of Jared how important it is to pray. Then Jesus helped the brother of Jared make a plan so his family and friends could cross the sea and get to the promised land.

It's important for us to pray too. When we pray and ask Jesus to bless us, He can help us make plans and get the things we need. The more we pray, the closer we feel to Jesus and the more we love Him.

Thought Question: What does it mean to pray always or to always have a prayer in your heart?

4. I LOVE JESUS MORE WHEN I READ THE SCRIPTURES

Pedro's grandma loves to do family history. Pedro used to think all of those old papers and records online looked boring. But then his grandma told him that as she read stories about their ancestors, she started to love them more and more.

The same thing is true about Jesus. When we read about Him in the scriptures, we start to love Him more and more. The stories in the scriptures teach us what Jesus is like. There are stories about Jesus growing up. There are stories about when He taught people on the earth. There are stories about the many miracles that He performed. And there are stories about how He died and was resurrected.

Every time we read about Jesus in the scriptures, our love for Him grows. And as we love Him more and more, we want to become more and more like Him.

Thought Question: What is your favorite scripture story about Jesus?

SCRIPTURE

And Jesus increased in wisdom and stature, and in favour with God and man.
—Luke 2:52

VISUAL AID

GAB 34
"Boy Jesus in the Temple"

ILLUSTRATION IDEAS

A boy, a grandma, a computer, Jesus, the scriptures

CHAPTER 10

EVERYONE *Can* COME *unto* CHRIST

"Yea, come unto Christ, and be perfected in him."—Moroni 10:32

1. PROPHETS LEAD US TO JESUS

SCRIPTURE

And they did harden their hearts from time to time, and they did revile against Moses, and also against God; nevertheless . . . they were led forth by his matchless power into the land of promise.
—1 Nephi 17:42

VISUAL AID

GAB 13
"Moses and the Burning Bush"

ILLUSTRATION IDEAS

Moses, the children of Israel, President Monson, Jesus

Moses was an important prophet. He led the children of Israel through the wilderness to the promised land.

Sometimes the children of Israel listened to Moses and did what he said. Other times, they complained and stopped listening. They made bad choices and didn't want to follow Moses. This made Moses sad and worried. He wanted the people to choose the right so they could live happily in the promised land.

Today, we have a prophet on the earth who has almost the same job as Moses. Our prophet, President Monson, doesn't lead us out in the wilderness. But he does try to help our spirits stay on the right path so we can return to live with Jesus someday.

It is a prophet's job to teach people about Jesus. Moses taught the children of Israel about Jesus and President Monson still teaches us about Jesus today.

Thought Question: Have you heard President Monson bear his testimony of Jesus? How did it make you feel?

2. WE CAN LEAD OTHERS TO JESUS

Leah loves going to Primary. She has a lot of fun learning lessons, singing songs, and playing games with her friends at church. Going to church makes Leah happy, and other people can see that.

At school, Leah's teacher noticed that Leah was honest and kind to other people. So the teacher asked Leah's mom what made Leah so happy and nice. Her mom explained that Leah was trying to be like Jesus, just as she had been taught at church.

Leah's teacher wanted to know more about the kinds of things Leah learned at church. Because Leah was a good example, her teacher got to learn more about Jesus.

We can all be good examples and help others want to know more about Jesus. When we lead others to Jesus, they will be happier, and so will we.

Thought Question: What could you do to set a good example and lead others to Jesus?

SCRIPTURE

Let your light so shine before men, that they may see your good works, and glorify your father which is in heaven. —Matthew 5:16

VISUAL AID

GAB 110 "Missionaries: Sisters"

ILLUSTRATION IDEAS

A girl, a chapel, a teacher, Jesus

3. I CAN GROW CLOSER TO JESUS AS I REPENT

SCRIPTURE

That no unclean thing shall be permitted to come into thy house to pollute it; and when thy people transgress, any of them, they may speedily repent and return unto thee.
—D&C 109:20–21

VISUAL AID

GAB 117
"Kirtland Temple"

ILLUSTRATION IDEAS

A temple, Joseph Smith, Heavenly Father, Jesus

The people that lived in Kirtland worked hard to build a temple. They knew it would be the house of the Lord, a place where Heavenly Father and Jesus could be with the Saints. It took the people a long time to build the temple. But when they were done, it was beautiful.

Then Joseph Smith said a special prayer to dedicate the temple. Joseph prayed for many things. One of the things he prayed for was that nothing unclean would come into the temple. This is because Heavenly Father and Jesus are pure and clean. They can't be around things that are not clean. It just doesn't work.

That's why Jesus wants us to repent. When we repent, all the sins and bad thoughts we have had are forgiven and go away. After we repent, we are clean again, which means we can be close to Jesus and Heavenly Father once more.

Thought Question: Have you ever been to a temple open house or seen pictures of the inside of a temple?

4. MY FAMILY CAN RETURN TO JESUS BECAUSE OF TEMPLE WORK

Imagine a big key chain with lots of keys on it. Each one unlocks a different door. In the gospel, we perform special ordinances that are like keys. Being baptized is one of those ordinances. When we are baptized, it's like we are given a key that can help us unlock a door on our pathway back to Jesus and Heavenly Father.

In the temple, we perform more ordinances and we are given more keys. We need these ordinances in order to return to Jesus and Heavenly Father. Without them, we would be stuck. Just like being locked out of a door without the key.

That's why we go to the temple. There, we can get all the keys we need for ourselves and for the other people in our families. Once we have all these keys, we will be able to return to Jesus and live with Him and everyone we love forever.

Thought Question: What are some other ordinances that we need in order to return to live with Jesus?

SCRIPTURE

The dead who repent will be redeemed, through obedience to the ordinances of the house of God.
—D&C 138:58

VISUAL AID

GAB 121
"Temple Baptismal Font"

ILLUSTRATION IDEAS

A key, a keychain, a person being baptized, the temple, a family

CHAPTER 11

I Can SERVE GOD by SERVING OTHERS

"When ye are in the service of your fellow beings ye are only in the service of your God."—Mosiah 2:17

1. JESUS KNEW HOW TO LOVE AND SERVE

SCRIPTURE

This beginning of miracles did Jesus in Cana of Galilee, and manifested forth his glory; and his disciples believed on him.
—John 2:11

VISUAL AID

GAB 33
"Jesus Praying with His Mother"

ILLUSTRATION IDEAS

Jesus, Mary, water, wine, the governor

In Jesus's day, the people drank wine when they were celebrating instead of water. This wine wasn't bad for you the way wine is today. One time, Jesus went to a wedding with his family in a place called Cana. Jesus's mother, Mary, was helping with the wedding. After a little while, the people who were in charge of the wedding ran out of wine for their guests.

Mary knew what to do. She told Jesus that there was no more wine. Jesus loved His mother. He wanted to help. He had some men fill up six pots with water and then pour some of the water into a glass and give it to the most important wedding guest: the governor.

When the governor drank the water, he said it was the best wine he'd tasted at the party. Jesus had performed a miracle. He turned the water into wine because He loved Mary and He wanted to serve her.

Thought Question: Can you think of some more stories about Jesus helping people?

2. I CAN BE LIKE JESUS BY SERVING OTHERS

When Jesus visited the Nephites, He taught them many things. Then it came time for Him to leave. But the people were sad. They wanted Jesus to stay so they could spend more time with Him.

Jesus loved the people. He saw that they were sad, so He decided to stay longer. Then He used His power to heal the sick people and to bless all the children.

The kind of love that Jesus has is called charity. When we have charity, we don't think about ourselves all that much because we are too busy thinking about how to help other people.

It's important to have and practice charity because it helps us to become more like Jesus. Having charity means loving people, even if they are mean or angry or hurtful. Jesus loves everyone and that is how He wants us to love too.

Thought Question: What are some ways that you can show charity to the people around you?

SCRIPTURE

Have ye any that are sick among you? . . . Bring them hither and I will heal them, for I have compassion upon you; my bowels are filled with mercy.
—3 Nephi 17:7

VISUAL AID

GAB 84
"Jesus Blesses the Nephite Children"

ILLUSTRATION IDEAS

Jesus, the Nephites, a heart

3. I SERVE GOD BY SERVING MY FAMILY

SCRIPTURE

Honour thy father and thy mother: that thy days may be long upon the land which the Lord thy God giveth thee.
—Exodus 20:12

VISUAL AID

GAB 112
"Family Prayer"

ILLUSTRATION IDEAS

A boy, some toys, a table, socks and shoes

Ryan is a good helper. When he was little, his mom was sick. Ryan helped his mom by playing quietly with his toys and cleaning them up when he was done. Now he helps by doing other chores, like setting the table, wiping up spills, and putting his socks and shoes away.

All of us can help our families in different ways. You probably have your own chores that you can do to help. And you can help by being happy and kind to the people in your family. You could write a nice note or draw and color a picture for someone you love. You could even do something nice but keep it a secret so no one knows it was you.

Heavenly Father sent you to live with your family. He wants you to be nice to them and help them. When you serve the people in your family, you are helping Heavenly Father to bless them.

Thought Question: Can you remember the last time you helped someone in your family? What did you do?

4. I SERVE GOD BY SERVING MY NEIGHBORS

Eleanor is an actress. She loves to put on plays with her friends and dress up in fun costumes. Eleanor's mom likes to act too. One time, she and Eleanor decided to be in a big play together. They worked hard to memorize their lines and get ready for opening night. Finally, it was time to perform!

Lots of people came to see Eleanor's play. They loved watching her and her mom up on the stage. Eleanor made the audience laugh and entertained them with her singing.

In a way, when Eleanor was acting, she was giving service. She spent a long time preparing and making sure that the play would make people happy to see it. There are lots of ways we can give service. Often, it's easier than you'd think.

Heavenly Father gave Eleanor a talent for acting so that she could use her talent to help the people around her. You have talents, too, and when you use them to give service to others, you are also giving service to God.

Thought Question: How can you find opportunities to share your talents and serve in your community?

SCRIPTURE

Choose ye this day, to serve the Lord God who made you. —Moses 6:33

VISUAL AID

GAB 115 "Service"

ILLUSTRATION IDEAS

A girl, a mom, a stage, Heavenly Father

CHAPTER 12

JESUS, *My* REDEEMER, LIVES TODAY

"And now, after the many testimonies which have been given of him, this is the testimony, last of all, which we give of him: That he lives!"—D&C 76:22

1. JESUS WAS BORN IN BETHLEHEM, JUST AS PROPHETS FORETOLD

SCRIPTURE

And behold, he shall be born of Mary, at Jerusalem . . . she being a virgin, a precious and chosen vessel.
—Alma 7:10

VISUAL AID

GAB 22
"Isaiah Writes of Christ's Birth"

ILLUSTRATION IDEAS

Alma, Jesus, Mary, the scriptures

Alma lived many years before Jesus was born. Because Alma was a prophet, he wanted to know more about Jesus. He prayed to learn all that he could, and the Spirit revealed many things to him. Through the Spirit, Alma learned about Jesus's mother, Mary, and how special she would be. He also learned that Jesus would be a king, but He wouldn't live in a palace or a castle. Instead, He would live like a normal person and feel pain and sadness. Alma learned everything he could about Jesus. Then he told all of his friends and family what he had learned.

Many other prophets learned about Jesus too. They told the people what they knew and they wrote down the things they learned in books that eventually became the scriptures. Because so many prophets knew about Jesus, it was easier for the righteous people to recognize Jesus when He was born and know He was the Son of God.

Thought Question: Can you name any other prophets who testified of Jesus before He was born?

2. JESUS SAVED ALL OF US

The Zoramites had a rather strange church. Instead of believing in Jesus, they believed that Heavenly Father was only a spirit. They thought this spirit had chosen them to be the only special people and they would be the only ones who'd be saved.

Do you know what it means to be saved? It means that when we die, we can live again and be happy. The Zoramites thought that Heavenly Father only wanted to save them. But they were wrong. Jesus and Heavenly Father want to save everyone.

When Jesus died, He died for all of the people who have ever lived on the earth. He loves all people, even the ones who don't believe in Him, like the Zoramites. Because Jesus died for us, everyone will be able to live again. Everyone will have a body again. And that will make us all happy.

Thought Question: Will everyone who is resurrected live in the celestial kingdom?

SCRIPTURE

For behold, this is my work and my glory—to bring to pass the immortality and eternal life of man. —Moses 1:39

VISUAL AID

GAB 116 "Christ and Children from around the World"

ILLUSTRATION IDEAS

The Zoramites, Heavenly Father, Jesus, lots of people

3. SOMEDAY JESUS WILL COME BACK TO THE EARTH

SCRIPTURE

We believe . . . that Christ will reign personally upon the earth; and, that the earth will be renewed and receive its paradisiacal glory.
—Articles of Faith 1:10

VISUAL AID

GAB 66
"The Second Coming"

ILLUSTRATION IDEAS

Prophets, Jesus, a crown, the earth

Before Jesus was born, many people knew He would come. These people were prophets, and they told their family and friends about Jesus. They said He would be born in Bethlehem and He would die for our sins.

All of the things that the prophets said about Jesus actually happened. He was born in Bethlehem. And He did save us from our sins.

Many prophets have also seen the future. They have prophesied about the day Jesus will return to the earth. This time, He won't be born as a baby. He will come as a powerful king to rule in glory. All of the righteous people will be happy to see Him. The earth will be renewed so that it is more beautiful than it has ever been.

We can look forward to the day Jesus comes again. And we can help get ready for it by telling our family and friends about Jesus.

Thought Question: Do you know what signs will come before Jesus returns?

4. JESUS WANTS ME TO LIVE WITH HIM AGAIN

Eli's grandpa owned a farm. Eli loved to go visit his grandpa and help take care of the animals and fields. Sometimes, when they finished their chores, Eli's grandpa would drive them into town to get milkshakes. Eli loved his grandpa.

But one day, his grandpa got sick and died. Eli was so sad. His parents were sad too. But they knew that they would all be together again someday. Eli's family is sealed together. This means that even after they die, they will still be a family.

Jesus knows that the only way we can really be happy is for our whole family to be able to live with Him again. Eli's grandpa was a good man. Eli knows his grandpa is with Jesus again. Someday, Eli will return to Jesus too, and then he will be able to live with Jesus, his grandpa, and his whole family forever.

Thought Question: What do you need to do so that you can live with Jesus and your family forever?

SCRIPTURE

Sacred ordinances and covenants available in holy temples make it possible for individuals to return to the presence of God and for families to be united eternally. —The Family: A Proclamation to the World, paragraph 3

VISUAL AID

GAB 1
"Jesus Christ"

ILLUSTRATION IDEAS

A boy, a grandpa, a farm, milkshakes, a family, Jesus

Song Ideas

The following is a list of songs from the *Children's Songbook* that correspond to each talk. You can use them to reinforce the concepts taught in Primary that week. If your musical abilities are limited or you don't have access to an instrument, all of these songs are available at lds.org/music.

CHAPTER 1
1. I Am a Child of God, 2
   I Know My Father Lives, 5
2. He Sent His Son, 34
   This Is My Beloved Son, 76
3. A Child's Prayer, 12
   I Need My Heavenly Father, 18
   My Heavenly Father Loves Me, 228
4. Jesus Is Our Loving Friend, 58
   I Feel My Savior's Love, 74

CHAPTER 4

CHAPTER 5

CHAPTER 6

CHAPTER 7

CHAPTER 8

CHAPTER 9

CHAPTER 12

About the Author

Heidi Doxey has written five books in the Tiny Talks series. She graduated from BYU with a BA in English and a minor in editing. When she's not writing or reading, she loves riding her bike, going for walks, spending time with family and friends, and being outside.

She currently lives in Utah, where she works in publishing, but she still calls the San Francisco Bay Area home.

Heidi blogs at girlwithalltheanswers.blogspot.com, and you can find more info about the Tiny Talks series at TinyTalksBooks.com.

About the Illustrator

Corey Egbert has illustrated many books, including *The Holy Ghost Is like a Blanket* by Annalisa Hall and *Stars, Stockings & Shepherds* by Shersta Chabot. He lives in Virginia with his wife, Natalya; son, Oliver; and their cat, Rex.